creating beautiful

# WEDDING
# FLOWERS

# creating beautiful
# WEDDING FLOWERS

gorgeous ideas and 20 step-by-step projects for your big day

**Nancy Ursell**

**Antonia Swinson**

RYLAND
PETERS
& SMALL
LONDON NEW YORK

SENIOR DESIGNER Toni Kay
SENIOR EDITOR Clare Double
LOCATION RESEARCH Tracy Ogino
PRODUCTION Sheila Smith
ART DIRECTOR Anne-Marie Bulat
PUBLISHING DIRECTOR Alison Starling

PROJECTS Nancy Ursell
TEXT Antonia Swinson and Clare Double
STYLIST Liz Belton

First published in the UK in 2007 by
Ryland Peters & Small
519 Broadway, 5th Floor
New York, NY 10012
www.rylandpeters.com

10 9 8 7 6 5 4 3

Text, design, and photographs
© Ryland Peters & Small 2007

   Library of Congress Cataloging-in-Publication Data
Ursell, Nancy.
   Creating beautiful wedding flowers : gorgeous ideas
and 20 step-by-step projects for your big day / Nancy
Ursell, Antonia Swinson.
      p. cm.
   ISBN-13: 978-1-84597-334-6
   1. Wedding decorations. 2. Floral decorations. 3.
Handicraft. I. Swinson, Antonia. II. Title.
   SB449.5.W4U77 2007
   745.92'6–dc22
                              2006021641


Printed and bound in China.

# contents

# Introduction

Weddings and flowers are a happy marriage. The sheer joyous beauty of flowers is enough to merit their use on a day of romance and celebration. Such is the variety of plants available in markets, florists, and, if you're lucky, your own backyard, and such is the multitude of ways in which they can be arranged, that whatever style of wedding you're planning—grand, traditional, modern, informal—there will be flowers that look right and will enhance your enjoyment of the day. Nor need your floral decorations cost a fortune if you're working to a tight budget. Don't neglect the everyday flowers you'll find in gardens, such as irises, forget-me-nots, and hydrangeas. Go for what's in season and keep things simple and unpretentious, letting the beauty of even humble flowers speak for itself. Moreover, if you arrange the flowers for the wedding yourself (or with friends and family), you'll save money and have the fun and pleasure of creating something that's truly personal. This book is designed to help you do just this. If you're using a professional florist, there are inspirations and ideas to get you started on planning your floral scheme. If, however, you want to try it yourself, there are twenty projects that take you through the creative process step by step. Patience and care rather than professional skill are required, though it would be wise to practice the basic techniques in the months before the day. There are bouquets for the bride, accessories for the bridesmaids, boutonnières, corsages, table centerpieces, and floral details for the reception. The arrangements range from the classic to the strikingly contemporary and are versatile, elegant, and, above all, beautiful. Whatever you decide to make, from a single boutonnière for your groom to a centerpiece for the bride's table, enjoy what you do and take pleasure in the results on your wedding day.

# Flowers for the bride

Once a wedding date is set, one of the first things a bride's mind turns to is what she will wear. Buying the dress is a thrilling part of the wedding ritual, but the dress is only part of what makes a bride look special. There are the other details—shoes, headdress, and, of course, flowers. The natural beauty of flowers and the ancient associations which many of them have with love and fertility have meant that for hundreds of years brides have carried bouquets or posies, a symbol of the passage from old life to new.

# bridal bouquets

Handsome though a groom looks in his tuxedo or best suit, the bride is undeniably the star of the day, so the flowers she carries are also the focus of much attention. The wedding dress is usually the key stylistic element of the day, and its style, fabric, and color should help to shape ideas for the bouquet.

A traditional white or off-white dress is a flattering backdrop to flowers of any color, from white and pastels to strong reds or pinks. If the dress is a different color, whether the palest pink or blue or something more daring, the flowers need to be chosen with more care, to avoid an unflattering clash. White, with its quality of timeless elegance, is still the classic choice for the bouquet as much as for the dress. Pastel colors are easy to work with, feminine and romantic. Deeper colors—rich pinks, purples, deep blues, and sultry reds—require more thought but, judiciously handled, can look spectacular. Moreover, certain colors seem to lend themselves to the quality of light peculiar to each season:

**ABOVE LEFT** Charm and romance combine in this summer bouquet of flowers from an English garden—roses, stocks, scabious, carnations, lady's mantle, and stephanotis buds.

**ABOVE RIGHT** Pink is unashamedly feminine and a beautiful color to use with white. This large, extravagant bouquet, tied with a huge bronze-green bow, uses palest pink roses, lilies, jasmine, and kangaroo paw.

**BELOW LEFT** Sweet-scented lilac is a star shrub of late spring. Here, a large, informal bunch has been made with long stems of purple and white lilac.

**BELOW CENTER** The huge, feathery centers of these poppy anemones contrast dramatically with their soft, pink-flushed white petals to make an exceptionally pretty and elegant hand-tied bouquet. A collar of shimmering silver organza and a cranberry satin bow give the arrangement a glamorous finish.

**BELOW RIGHT** This beautifully simple bouquet is composed entirely of white roses. Tying the stems with blue organza ribbon creates a color link with touches on the bride's dress.

ABOVE This herb bouquet was inspired by Elizabethan posies (herbs were once thought to ward off evil). Here, rosemary, golden marjoram, thyme, sage, and tarragon offer a variety of scents and textures. The ribbon streamers are reminiscent of traditional maypoles.

LEFT This neat posy has been made in the formal Victorian style, with the flowers wired into concentric circles. The color scheme of lime green and soft blue—guelder rose, lisianthus, and scented hyacinths surrounded by galax leaves—gives it a soft and more modern look.

BELOW This sophisticated posy is composed of silky-petaled gloxinias (buy this conservatory plant in garden centers) and hyacinths, surrounded by variegated hosta leaves.

dark reds and greens in the pale light of winter; blue, white, and yellow in spring; bright colors in the strong sunlight of summer; and mellow oranges, golds, and yellows in the fall.

Think about the shape you'd like your bouquet to be. The most traditional is a teardrop or "shower" shape, with all the flowers individually wired, creating a fairly formal look. Very popular currently are hand-tied bouquets. Whether you choose a large, loose bouquet or a small, domed posy will depend on the dress; don't let the flowers dominate the ensemble. For instance, with a classic but understated dress, a posy of lily of the valley might strike the right note. For a wedding in

A bunch of bright and cheerful country flowers, including sunflowers, clover, bachelor's buttons, buttercups, and bergamot, tied with deep-blue ribbon, is the perfect choice for a summer wedding in the country.

FAR LEFT A bouquet of grape hyacinths and bachelor's buttons shows how beautiful these simple garden flowers can look.

LEFT Dramatic, sophisticated black and white is created here with poppy anemones, ranunculus, and roses, encircled with galax leaves.

bridal bouquets 13

Deeper colors—rich pinks, purples, deep blues, and sultry reds—can look spectacular.

**ABOVE LEFT** With its pale orange, lanternlike flowers and slender leaves, sandersonia is an unusual but elegant choice for a wedding. Here, the stems have simply been gathered into a large bunch and tied with a wide bronze organza ribbon.

**ABOVE CENTER** This dramatic bunch of tropical blooms—heliconias and ginger lilies, framed by palm leaves—sizzles with spicy color and is as far removed from a traditional bouquet as it's possible to get.

**ABOVE RIGHT** This neat, feminine bouquet celebrates spring with mimosa and scented Yellow Cheerfulness narcissi. Pretty braid, secured with pearl-headed pins, binds the long stems, making this bouquet particularly easy to hold.

**RIGHT** Iceland poppies make a bouquet of unconventional, fragile beauty. The flowers have fine, papery petals and come in colors ranging from white to yellows, oranges, and reds.

**TOP** Red is a glamorous counterpoint to a white wedding dress, as demonstrated by this bouquet of Lipstick and Grand Prix roses.

**ABOVE** This large, loose bouquet is all about color, with Naranja and Decca roses, Iceland poppies, and ranunculus creating a fabulous melange of burnt orange and golden yellow.

**LEFT** The charm of lily of the valley, combined with exquisite scent, makes it a classic choice.

ABOVE LEFT Red roses are a symbol of love the world over, and here, two varieties—Tamango and Grand Prix—have been partnered with skimmia leaves and flowers and a collar of sheer burgundy fabric to produce a very striking and sophisticated bouquet.

ABOVE This bouquet captures the rich and mellow shades of fall with kumquats, Cape gooseberries, hypericum (St. John's wort) berries, roses, and papery autumn leaves.

LEFT Designed for a bride and her two adult attendants, these neat little posies of tightly furled ranunculus in orange, pink, and maroon are chic and modern, making them ideal for a city-hall ceremony.

OPPOSITE ABOVE This intensely colored bouquet has more than a hint of the tropics about it, thanks to its daring combination of red and gold glory lilies, bright pink sweet peas, and roses in soft pink, black-red, and ruby red, interspersed with skimmia leaves.

the country, the bride might choose a generous bunch of scented garden roses, peonies, and stocks. A bouquet of lilies might be the perfect partner for a grand dress and a chic metropolitan wedding. With a sleek column dress, a sheaf of sculptural flowers, such as calla lilies or ginger lilies, could be the answer.

Think about the flowers themselves and whether you want a bouquet composed of one type—such as roses or ranunculus—or a mixture. Many flowers—among them tulips, carnations, lilies, and roses—are available all year,

This dressy bouquet was created with an evening reception in mind and strikes a glamorous note. Sumptuous Black Beauty roses are mixed with purple and shocking-pink sweet peas, and white and burgundy ranunculus.

## Ribbon, braid, and fabric can all be used to give a bouquet a fairy-tale bridal finish.

but it's also nice to take advantage of seasonal specialties. In spring, there are narcissi and hyacinths; in summer, peonies, sweet peas, and stocks; in the fall, hydrangeas and chrysanthemums; in winter, camellias and amaryllis.

Finally, ribbon, braid, and fabric can all be used to give a bouquet a fairy-tale bridal finish. Stems can be bound with ribbon and secured prettily with pearl-headed pins, or criss-crossed with ornate braid. Sheer fabrics can be swathed around a bouquet to form a collar, and ribbon can be fashioned into extravagant multilooped bows or streamers.

**FAR LEFT** This sheaf of pure white calla lilies is magnificent in its sculptural simplicity. The flowers are so glorious that they speak for themselves and need no further embellishment than a length of wide, pewter ribbon.

**LEFT** Frivolity and fun characterize this joyously colorful bouquet. Combining such strong colors requires skill and a judicious blending of deep and paler shades, achieved here with white-and-pink camellias, dark purple sweet peas, and pink and orange-to-lime green ranunculus, finished with burgundy net and multicolored ribbons.

**ABOVE** The classic white or cream wedding dress is the perfect counterfoil for strong color, so this could be the occasion to choose flowers that will really make a statement. Red and green are opposites on the color wheel, making them a visually arresting partnership. For this bouquet, the effect of the combination has been heightened with sharp lime green in the form of lady's mantle and sultry black-red in the form of Black Beauty roses, along with bright red Lipstick roses.

**LEFT** Unashamedly romantic and feminine, pink is a favorite for weddings. Pastel shades are popular, but why not try something with more intensity? These cerise Singapore orchids, flushed with white, are small and delicate but utterly beguiling and glamorous. Here, they've been gathered into a little bunch, their stems bound in ruched satin trimming.

**OPPOSITE BELOW** This cool and calm bouquet combines exotic and cottage-garden flowers—cymbidium orchids, kangaroo paw, galax leaves, and the frothy heads of lady's mantle.

# country-style bouquet

Once mastered, the spiral technique used for this bouquet can be employed to produce all sorts of hand-tied bunches, large or small. Its domed shape shows all the blooms to best advantage and gives the finished arrangement a full, densely packed look. The result here is soft, romantic, and relaxed, the flowers those you might find in a well-stocked country garden. The color palette of white, pastel pink, and warm pink is fresh and feminine, an effect reinforced by the delicacy of the flower heads and lavender foliage. Scent plays an important role in this bouquet, and the sweet hyacinths and aromatic lavender will exude their perfume over the course of the wedding, particularly on a warm day. Plain sheer ribbon, tied in a simple bow, finishes the bouquet in unfussy but pretty style.

**FLOWERS & MATERIALS**
*3 white hyacinths*
*handful long-stemmed ruscus foliage*
*5 pink bouvardia*
*6 white alliums*
*4 pink snapdragons*
*handful of lavender*

*oasis tape*
*scissors*
*ribbon*

1   Remove the lower leaves from the plants. When you come to the snapdragon, remove most of the flowers, leaving only the tightly packed blooms at the end of the stem. Remove the hyacinth leaves, but leave the root end intact.

2   Start with a hyacinth. Add a stem of foliage and a bouvardia from right to left, under the hyacinth. Make the binding point (where you hold the flowers) quite high, as shown, because the fleshy hyacinth stem may droop if held lower.

3   Continue by adding an allium and a snapdragon, from right to left as before. Add the stems in a roughly spiral formation to show off every flower. Keep the flower heads at the same level. This will give the finished bouquet a well-packed look.

4   Add more foliage and add the first stem of lavender, continuing to spiral the stems as you work. Hyacinths can droop quickly if they are over-warmed by your hands, so try not to hold the hyacinth stems too firmly or too long.

5  Add one more of each flower in the same order, including some extra lavender for fragrance. Pause here to check the shape of your bouquet and to make sure none of the flowers is crushed. Support the hyacinth with one hand.

6  Use the remaining flowers and foliage, this time not in any particular order but where you think the extra stems will look best and give a balanced bouquet. Aim for an informal effect, as if the bouquet has been picked from a garden.

7  When you are satisfied with the appearance of your bouquet, bind the stems firmly with oasis tape. Next, measure a hand and a half's width below the flowers, as shown, and trim the ends neatly at that point.

8  Wrap your chosen ribbon around the stems several times, making sure the tape is concealed. Tie a double knot and finish with a large bow. Keep the bouquet in water in a cool place until needed.

# pastel bouquet

The flowers included here—roses, stocks, and freesias—are time-honored favorites with florists because they're adaptable, readily available and, above all, beautiful. The delicious mixture of cream, white, and pink is hard to beat, but the pink roses could be replaced with another variety in a soft shade, such as pale yellow or apricot, to suit the day's color scheme. The stocks and freesias will give off their delicious scent during the day, something the bride can appreciate at close quarters. The wired rhinestone decorations add a discreet touch of glamour to the arrangement and would be particularly suitable if the bride were wearing a beaded wedding dress or bejeweled tiara. The pearl-headed pins securing the ribbon are a final feminine detail.

**FLOWERS & MATERIALS**

*8 pink Sweet Akito roses*
*6 white Akito roses*
*6 cream Vendella roses*
*5 cream stocks*
*15 white freesias*

*scissors*
*knife*
*ready-wired rhinestone decorations (optional)*
*florist's tape*
*string*
*oasis tape*
*ribbon*
*3 pearl-headed pins*

1 Remove any thorns and leaves from the flowers. If you are using rhinestone decorations, add them to a few of the roses. Holding the stone level with the rose head, wrap the wire around the stem. Wind florist's tape over the wire to fix.

2 Take a flower in your left hand, about 4 in (10 cm) down the stem. (Always hold firmly at this binding point.) Place another behind it, from right to left at a slight angle. Go on, alternating varieties. Turn the bouquet a little each time.

3 When you add the freesias, place them so their heads turn out. When you have used half the flowers, check that the bouquet's shape is slightly domed. (Standing in front of a mirror will make this easier.) Add the remaining flowers.

4 Once you are happy with the design, make sure you keep your hand firmly at the binding point. Clamp the end of the string under your thumb and wind around the stems several times. Cover with oasis tape to secure the shape.

5   To measure the correct length for the bouquet's stems, keep holding the bouquet with one hand and move your other hand down a half-hand length. Cut the flower stems at this point, making the ends blunt.

6   When the stems are cut, the bouquet should stand alone, with the stems spiraled attractively. You may have to trim a few ends again before your bouquet will stand up. (Note: the stems should be closely packed.)

7   Secure the end of your chosen ribbon with oasis tape, then wrap the ribbon around the stems to hide all the tape and string. Anchor the ribbon with three pearl-headed pins, set in a vertical line down the stem.

8   Keep the bouquet in water until an hour or two before required (take it out not less than an hour before). Dry the stems well with paper towels. After your big day, the bouquet should last a week in water, in cool conditions.

# long-stemmed bouquet

This elegant bouquet uses plants with a sculptural quality—fluted calla lilies and bladelike bear grass. Staggering the lilies so they're not compressed into a bunch gives the arrangement a fluted shape, reinforcing the graceful curves of the lilies. This and the grass balance out the extra-long stems, producing an exaggerated silhouette that would be an effective complement to a dress with equally long lines, such as a column style. The beads look like dew drops and soften the severity of the bear grass.

### FLOWERS & MATERIALS
*5 calla lilies*
*bear grass*

*scissors*
*oasis tape*
*small clear beads*
*ribbon*
*thin silver wire*

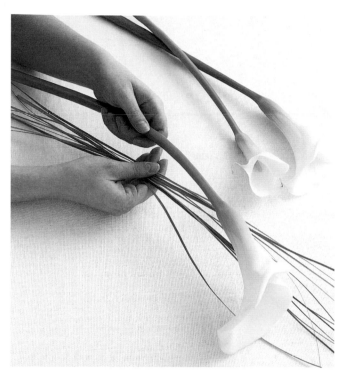

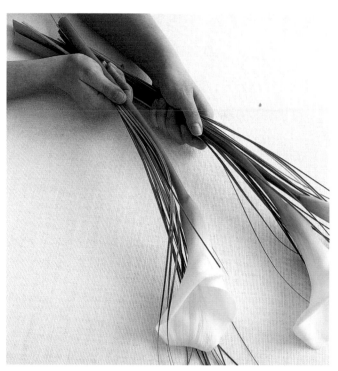

1 Carefully warm the lily stems with your hands. This will make them flexible enough to give a graceful arching shape to the bouquet. Take a small bunch of bear grass in your right hand and place the largest lily on top with your left.

2 Add two more bunches, using the next largest lilies. Add from the right and lay the lily on top or from the left, going under. Place each lower, so the flowers are visible. Make your binding point two-thirds of the way down the stem.

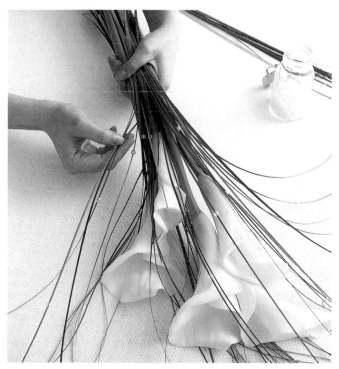

3 Add the last two lilies and secure with oasis tape. Thread one clear bead onto several individual strands of bear grass, at a variety of heights so the bouquet will sparkle all over. Add these strands to the bouquet and bind with oasis tape.

4 Trim the ends, leaving them long, and wind ribbon down the stems, overlapping slightly each time. Pin at the back and wrap silver wire around. Finally, add beads to the wire and twist the wire closed at the back. Tuck ends into the ribbon.

# teardrop bouquet

This arrangement is fairly demanding to make, involving wiring rather than tying the flowers. If you try it, practice the wiring technique before you attempt the bouquet itself. Success also depends on getting the teardrop shape perfect, so it's vital that you start with the right oasis bouquet holder. The choice of flowers used here puts the emphasis firmly on color, with deep and pale pink, lilac, and purple, though it would look just as beautiful with a selection of white flowers. The bouquet is created precisely and painstakingly, yet there is a sense of looseness and movement about it, as if the flowers were tumbling out of the bride's hands. As an alternative to the foliage used here, you could try trailing jasmine or honeysuckle, to heighten the bouquet's romantic look.

**FLOWERS & MATERIALS**
*8 large pale pink Akito roses*
*6 stems pale and dark lilac dendrobium orchid*
*10 stems pink veronica*
*8 dark pink Ballet roses*
*ruscus foliage*
*asparagus fern*

*old block of oasis*
*oasis tape*
*ready-made oasis bouquet holder with handle*
*(the one we used contained an oasis*
*4 in (10 cm) from top to bottom)*
*scissors*
*thick wires*

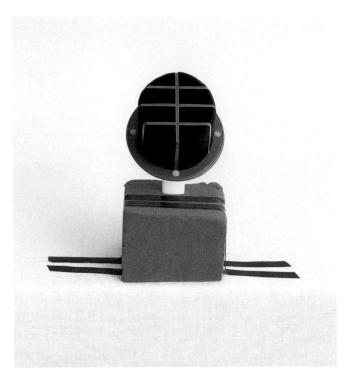

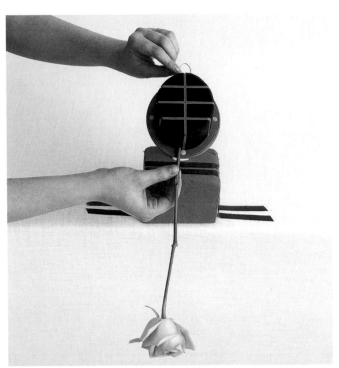

**1** Tape a dry oasis block to the edge of your work surface. Soak the oasis bouquet holder and stick it firmly into the dry block, at an angle to give you a view of the top and sides. This will hold the bouquet in place while you work.

**2** Trim a pale pink rose stem to about 8 in (20 cm). Wire it with a long single-leg mount (see page 74, step 2). Insert the rose tip into the oasis where shown. When the wire emerges at the top, loop the end over and secure in oasis.

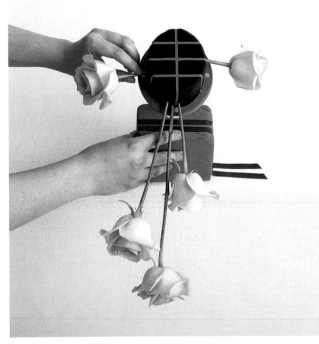

**3** Repeat step 2 for two more trailing roses, at different heights as shown. Cut two stems about 3 in (8 cm) long and insert either side of the oasis, halfway up. There is no need to wire these, as they are lighter than the lower roses.

**4** Cut three short stems, about 2½ in (6 cm). Place one center top (to face the bride) and two on the front of the holder as shown. Don't place them in a straight line; the pale pink roses should form a sort of S shape from top to bottom.

5 Wire the orchid stems as you did the roses. Start inserting them from the bottom, again securing the wires with a loop. Fill the base and right side as shown, using all the stems and any smaller pieces (you don't need to wire these).

6 Cut the veronica stems and add them as you did the orchids. Wire stems that will hang down and use the rest of the veronica to fill the left side of the arrangement. A round top and falling teardrop shape should become apparent.

7 Insert the dark pink roses to fill gaps in the bouquet. Take care just to push the tip of each rose into the oasis; an over-stuffed oasis can crumble. If you keep the stems short, you should not need to wire these roses.

8 Cut ruscus tips, leaving three or four leaves. Use them to fill the oasis at the top and form a "collar," covering any wires. Use the fern fronds and any leftover flowers to soften the bouquet's edges and fill any holes. No oasis should show.

# winter wedding bouquet

Many flowers are available all year, making summery bouquets possible in the depths of winter. However, summer flowers can look inappropriate in the cool, thin light and low temperatures of winter, and it's often more effective to choose something that reflects the season. This glamorous bouquet is a clever compromise. Roses flower naturally all summer, but the colors used here—sultry black-red and intense ruby, combined with the dark forest green of the aspidistra leaves—are quintessentially wintry, the colors of holly and berries. This densely packed, domed bouquet shows off the intricate shape and velvety texture of the rose heads to perfection, and the gleaming leaves—folded over to resemble the loops of a huge silk bow—reinforce the arrangement's lavish look.

**FLOWERS & MATERIALS**

*10 aspidistra leaves*
*15 deep red Black Baca roses*
*15 red Grand Prix roses*

*green string*
*scissors*
*oasis tape*
*ribbon*

1 Wipe the aspidistra leaves clean. If desired, apply leaf shine or a little cooking oil to give them a sheen. Take one leaf and fold the tip back on itself to meet the stem. Tie securely with string. Repeat for the remaining leaves.

2 Strip all the roses of leaves and thorns to leave clean, smooth stems. Take the first Black Baca rose in your right hand and feed it behind the first red rose, held in your left hand. Hold the stems at the binding point.

3 Keeping the roses in your left hand, clamp one end of the string under your left thumb. Use your right hand to tie the roses together, making sure the flower heads are level. Do not cut the string.

4 Repeat this process to add most of the roses (you don't need to go in color order), keeping the heads level. Wrap the string around about every three roses, to keep them in position. Don't go too tightly, so you can tweak them later.

5 When you get to the last eight roses, add them to the bouquet slightly lower than the others, to give a dome shape to the arrangement. Tie off the string and cut, then cover and secure it with oasis tape.

6 Add the aspidistra leaves to make a decorative collar for the flowers. The front of the leaf and stem should face the flowers (the string tie will be hidden by ribbon). Add each leaf behind the last and slightly overlapping, as shown.

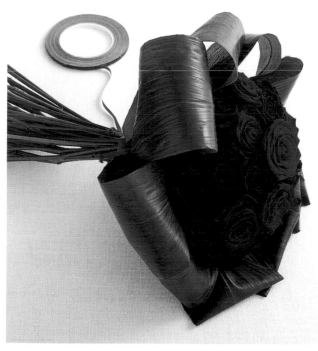

7 You may need to adjust the leaves slightly so they are evenly spaced around the bouquet. Tie all the leaves to the bouquet with string, then secure with oasis tape. The leaves should frame the flowers without squashing them.

8 Cut the stems about a hand and a half's width down from the string. Keep them even for a neat appearance. Finish the bouquet with ribbon of your choice. We wrapped the ribbon around several times and finished with a bow.

# romantic bouquet

White is, of course, the classic wedding color, for flowers as much as for dresses, a timelessly elegant choice for a bouquet at any time of year. For this one, a variety of white flowers has been used to guarantee an interesting array of shape and texture; the lilac, moreover, is beautifully perfumed. The eucalyptus foliage is a subtle gray-green, giving a softer look to the arrangement than dark green foliage would, and its small leaves are delicate and aromatic. The romantic mood of the bouquet is carried through to the arrangement of the flowers themselves, not in the spiral formation often used for tied bunches but in a flatter, fanned shape. This is because the bouquet is designed to be carried gracefully over the arm in a charmingly traditional and feminine gesture.

**FLOWERS & MATERIALS**

*4 large heads of white lilac*
*8 white Akito roses*
*8 stems lysimachia*
*2 large bunches eucalyptus*

*oasis tape*
*scissors*
*knife (or pruners)*
*transparent wire-edged ribbon*
*pearl-headed pins*

1   Strip the lower leaves from the flowers and foliage. When
    you come to the eucalyptus (above), wash it before use, as
    it can leave a sticky residue on your hands. Leave about
    8 in (20 cm) of leaves on the end of each stem.

2   Start with the best stem of lilac. This will be the focal point.
    Begin to add the roses, lysimachia, and eucalyptus, keeping
    the binding point about a third of the way down the stems.
    Keep the flowers flat (not bunched) so they can all be seen.

3   This bouquet is designed to be carried over the arm, so,
    as you add more flowers and foliage, do so from the front.
    Keeping the stems straight (not spiraled) will give you
    a flat-backed shape that is easier to carry.

4   Create a fan shape, with flowers above and below your lilac
    focal point. When you are halfway through, check that you
    have built up the shape evenly on both sides and adjust as
    necessary. If you add more lilac now, do so from the back.

5   Fill in the back and sides of the bouquet with extra stems of eucalyptus. This will give a soft shape to the design, with most of the flowers at the front. The eucalyptus also contributes a wonderful scent.

6   Secure with oasis tape and trim the ends. Leave the stems longer than you would for a bouquet that will be held upright. If the lilac stems are very thick and woody, you may need to cut them with a knife or pruners.

7   Check that there are no snags on the stems that could damage the sleeves of the bride's dress. Secure with a loose, generous bow of transparent wire-edged ribbon. Leave long ends to give the design a soft, romantic look.

8   Finish the ribbon by anchoring the bow with pearl-headed pins. Keep the bouquet in water until the last minute, in cool conditions, or the lilac may suffer. You could also make smaller versions to be carried upright by the bridesmaids.

# Flowers for attendants

The bridesmaids' flowers must harmonize with the bride's, but not outshine them. For adult bridesmaids, the options run from posies to hair accessories, whether traditional, modern, full-blown, or minimal. Old-fashioned charm is often the favored look for little girls—floral circlets, posies with ribbon streamers, and floral balls finished with satin bows. For the very young, practicality is the key: keep accessories and arrangements comfortable and easy to hold, and give them to their recipients at the last minute, to avoid damage to fragile blooms.

**LEFT** At a romantic country wedding, white is the predominant color, accented with blue and deep pink. This young bridesmaid's posy uses roses, snowberries, bupleurum, stocks, freesias, and margaritas to evoke the glory of summer.

# bridesmaids' blooms

It's appropriate for the bridesmaids' flowers to be discernibly different from the bride's, making sure they complement hers without running any risk of overshadowing them. They should adhere to the same broad color and floral scheme, but there's no reason why they shouldn't offer an interesting variation on the theme. For instance, if the bridal bouquet is white roses bound with pink satin ribbon, the bridesmaids might carry posies of white sweet peas or lilies of the valley; or posies of small, pale pink spray roses, this time tied with

**LEFT** This beautiful bouquet for a bridesmaid pairs exquisite pink roses with palest pink hydrangea heads.

**BELOW LEFT** Daffodils, miniature narcissi, guelder rose, spring snowflakes, ranunculus, and senecio, tied with yellow gingham ribbon, capture the essence of spring.

**BELOW** More stars of spring make up these charming green bouquets. The bride's bouquet includes hellebores, Singapore orchids, proteas, guelder rose, and laurustinus. The little girls' posies include many of the same flowers. One has been given a ruff of ivy leaves, while the other has been arranged in the Victorian style (see page 12).

**RIGHT** This bridesmaid's bouquet is straight from a country garden, with lupines, roses, stocks, sweet peas, old-fashioned pinks, and ripening blackberries.

**CENTER AND BELOW RIGHT** These floral hair accessories have been made by painstakingly wiring blooms onto a hairband and a wide hairslide.

white ribbon. If the bride's bouquet is an array of white and deep pink roses, stocks, carnations, and scabious, the bridesmaids' bouquets might use carnations only, in paler tones of pink interspersed with white.

It's usual for attendants, whether adult or young, to carry smaller arrangements than the bride's. It's particularly important for little girl attendants that their flowers are easy to carry—light, neat, and with stems long enough for small hands to hold tightly. Moreover, there are all sorts of alternatives to the traditional posy or bunch, such as wicker baskets or pretty bags filled with flowers, which turn into attractive keepsakes to take home after the day. Young bridesmaids could carry hoops (found in

**TOP** This bridesmaid's bouquet is based on the bride's. It brims with pink lilies, roses, jasmine, and photinia leaves. Bronze ribbon ties the long stems.

**ABOVE** Few things look more charming on a flower girl than a circlet of flowers, here composed predominantly of roses and bachelor's buttons.

**CENTER** Hydrangeas bloom late and are useful for late summer or fall weddings. Here, pink blooms are framed by their own leaves and tied with ribbon.

**ABOVE RIGHT** The rich, jewellike colors of poppy anemones make a lavish, romantic crown for a young flower girl in a simple white dress.

Floral headdresses have fairy-tale charm and work on young and adult attendants. Circlets and floral Alice bands look enchanting on little girls.

True blue is a rare color in the plant world, but these mophead hydrangeas are the deep azure of a summer sky. They've been wired into circlets and made into balls, decorated with powder blue and sapphire blue ribbon handles and streamers.

**THIS PAGE** Daisies are emblematic of childhood. This pompomlike variety is sold as summer bedding in garden centers. The white, pink, and blue heads almost look like candy and have been mixed with ivy leaves and forget-me-nots to make circlets and domed posies.

**OPPOSITE LEFT** These red bouquets are a sophisticated, striking choice. Both the bride and bridesmaid's arrangements consist of roses in subtly varying shades of red, spiked with white and green—photinia flowers and leaves for the bride, skimmia for the bridesmaid—to break up what could be an overwhelming effect.

most toy stores), bound with ribbon and entwined with flowers and foliage; or floral balls, made by inserting wired flowers (and even beads or feather butterflies) into a sphere of florist's foam. Floral headdresses have fairy-tale charm and work on young and adult attendants alike. Circlets and floral Alice bands look enchanting on little girls; for bridesmaids, flowers wired onto hairbands or slides give a more sophisticated look.

**ABOVE RIGHT** This sheaf of smoky eggplant and snowy white calla lilies, tied with steel grass, is daring and dramatic in its use of color and form. With their extraordinary fluted shape, these flowers aren't the choice for everyone, but in the right setting, and partnering the right gown, they can look spectacular.

**RIGHT** Proving that simple is often the most beautiful, this delicious posy of ice-cream pink hydrangeas echoes the decoration on the wedding cake.

**BELOW RIGHT** On a summer's day, blue and white is dazzling. Palest blue ribbon streamers hang from this flower girl's posy of roses, bachelor's buttons, and blue-green eucalyptus leaves, which give an aromatic scent in the heat.

# PROJECT 7
# flower girls' bags

These chic little bags, brimming with full-blown roses, are an ingenious alternative to a posy. The pastel blooms and tall bags used here look particularly pretty, but this project is open to all sorts of variations. For a winter wedding, red velvet bags and cream or white roses or camellias would look stylish; and in spring, narcissi or carnations could be used in place of roses. Don't be tempted to use a mixture of flowers or colors for the bags—they have most impact if each one uses a single variety in a single color.

### FLOWERS & MATERIALS
*cream Vendella roses, or to tone with your chosen bag*
*(we used 9 roses for an oasis block 3 x 2 in, 8 x 5 cm)*

*oasis block*
*knife*
*plastic wrap*
*small decorative bag (Note: wet oasis can*
*make a bag heavy for a flower girl)*
*scissors*

1 Soak the oasis in cold water for one minute, until all the air bubbles have dispersed. Cut the wet block to fit in the bag so that about 1¾ in (4 cm) of oasis shows above the top of the bag. Use oasis trimmings to raise the block, if needed.

2 Wrap the wet oasis in plastic wrap, folding any excess underneath to leave the top smooth. If the bag is not waterproof, line the inside with plastic wrap. Cut rose stems at an angle, leaving about 3 in (8 cm) to push into the oasis.

3 Insert the first rose at an almost horizontal angle so the flower rests gently over the bag's edge. Puncture the plastic wrap with scissors if necessary. Consider your bag's design; we began by placing a bloom in the center of one handle.

4 Continue around the edge of the oasis block and finish with two roses in its center. Place the roses close enough together to cover the oasis. The top of your bag should be filled with roses, leaving no oasis visible.

# a bridesmaid's feather posy

Ranunculuses are extraordinarily beautiful. Their heads are reminiscent of roses, but they have many more petals, all tightly curled. They come in wonderful colors, including white (often flushed with pink), orange with a lime-green center, shocking pink, and purple. Here, a dramatic dark plum variety is strikingly combined with snowy white feathers. This sophisticated posy would work well at a winter wedding. It's full of textural interest, the clustered flower heads set off by the airy lightness of the feathers.

## FLOWERS & MATERIALS

*10 plum ranunculus (this makes a small posy; you can use more flowers to create a larger bouquet)*

*thin wires*
*white synthetic feathers (about 16)*
*gutta tape*
*scissors*
*oasis tape • ribbon*

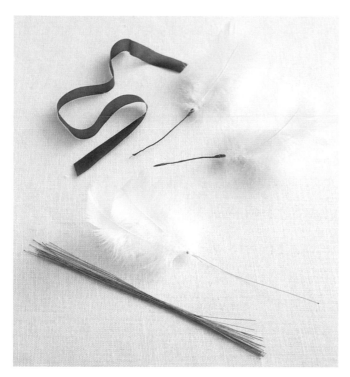

1 Wire the feathers with single-leg mounts (see page 74, step 2), in pairs to save time. Keep the wires long, about 3 in (8 cm), to make binding the feathers into the bouquet easier. Wind gutta tape around the wire to cover completely.

2 Arrange the flowers in a hand-tied bunch, placing each flower behind the last at an angle, from right to left. Turn the bouquet a little each time. Secure with oasis tape (not string, which may cut through the fleshy stems).

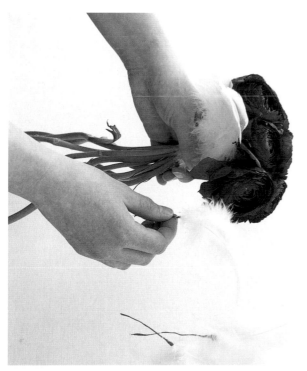

3 Place the wired feathers evenly around the posy, making sure the feather tips are level with the flowers. Aim to create a feathery collar around the flowers, with no gaps. Bind the feathers on with oasis tape.

4 Cut the ranunculus evenly to leave short stems. Tie ribbon around the posy to conceal all the wires, and finish with a bow. (If you cut the wires shorter before you do this, make sure any sharp points are covered by the ribbon.)

# floral ball

Floral balls are ideal for flower girls to carry, because they're light and easy
to hold. They have their origins in traditional decorations such as pomanders
and possess the old-fashioned charm of a Kate Greenaway illustration.
They take time to make but require more in the way of care and patience
than professional skill, especially if you use flowers with a stiff stem (such as
roses or carnations), which can be pushed straight into the foam ball without
being wired. The hypericum berries are useful for filling in any gaps and are
also pretty, looking almost like beads or pearls. The white color scheme shown
here is a classic, suits-all one, but roses in another color, such as soft pink,
apricot, or pale yellow, could be used.

**FLOWERS & MATERIALS**
*about 30 white Eskimo roses*
*about 15 smaller Vivianne spray roses*
*hypericum berries*

*oasis ball 3½ in (9 cm) in diameter*
*plastic wrap*
*scissors*
*thick wire*
*ribbon*
*water spray*

*Note: the ball will drip water as you insert the flowers,
so place newspaper on the floor as you work.*

1   Soak the oasis ball and wrap it in plastic wrap. Gather the wrap together at one point, twist firmly, and cut off the excess. Wind wire around the ball (holding the wrap in place), twist the ends, and poke them down into the oasis.

2   Wrap a second piece of wire around the ball, as shown. Secure the ends by tucking them under the first piece of wire and then firmly down into the oasis. Make sure there are no wire ends to cut little fingers.

3   Thread ribbon under one wire, opposite the plastic wrap twist, and secure with a single knot. Leave the ends very long so you can hang up the ball to work on it. The finished handle on our ball was 12 in (30 cm) long.

4   Hang up the ball; we used a chair. Cut the white rose stems short with angled tips. Insert two at the top of the ball to hide the ribbon knot, and two at the bottom, as shown. If necessary, pierce the plastic wrap with scissors first.

5  Insert more roses so you have completed a full circle, joining the roses you inserted at step 4. Now add more roses to form a circle in the opposite direction. You will need to turn the ball slightly to access the whole surface.

6  Add the rest of the larger roses to fill in the remaining quarters of oasis. Next, take the spray roses and cut the stems short at an angle. Position them all over the ball in any spaces between the larger roses.

7  Cut small sprays of hypericum berries. Insert them all over the ball, to fill any remaining gaps and provide an even spread of color contrast over the ball. No oasis should be visible on the finished ball.

8  Mist the finished ball with water to keep it fresh. To prevent the flowers from being crushed, keep it hanging or store on tissue paper in a cool place. When needed, cut the ribbon to the desired length, knot firmly and tie a bow for a handle.

## PROJECT 10
# orchid hair accessory

Few things look as pretty and romantic as fresh flowers in your hair. For a bridesmaid (or the bride), this orchid-covered hair comb is easy to make and looks exquisite, thanks to the beautiful form and color of the blooms used. It's important to use flowers that last really well once cut, since they need to look fresh all through the day. With their thick, waxy petals, cymbidium orchids fit the bill perfectly, but you could try other members of the family, such as moth orchids or Singapore orchids.

**FLOWERS & MATERIALS**

*spray of pink cymbidium orchid*

*scissors*
*hot glue gun and glue stick*
*hair comb or barrette*
*(we used a comb 3 in, 8 cm wide)*

1  Select the three best flower heads from the cymbidium (you will need more if you are using a larger hair accessory). Cut them off the main stem, leaving as much stalk as possible on the flower. This will make the flower easier to handle.

2  Heat the glue gun (cold glue will not work effectively) and put a dab of glue on each flower at the junction of the flower and its stalk. If you have not used a glue gun before, practice on something soft first, such as fabric.

3  Only apply glue to the top of each flower, leaving the teeth of the comb free to slide into the hair. Glue the flowers to the hair accessory so they face slightly downward. Start with the central flower, then fit the others snugly next to it.

4  When the glue has dried, cut the stems flush with the edge of the hair accessory. It can be kept overnight in a dark place. When needed, insert carefully into the hair, trying not to handle the blooms too much.

# Boutonnières and corsages

The practice of wearing a flower in the lapel can be traced back to medieval times, when knights wore their ladies' colors as love tokens. It's rare nowadays to wear boutonnières or corsages, but what could be a more appropriate occasion than a wedding? Think of these arrangements as miniature bouquets and you'll realize that there's plenty of scope for creativity with flowers, foliage, and finishing touches such as braid.

# for the bridal party

A boutonnière is often the only decorative accessory worn by the groom and other male members of the bridal party, introducing a welcome splash of color and marking them out as special on the day. Originally, the practice was for the groom to take a bloom directly from the bride's bouquet, and although boutonnières should complement the bride's flowers, they needn't replicate them. For instance, if the bridal bouquet is white lilies, the boutonnières might be white roses instead; or if the bouquet is composed mainly of pink ranunculus, the boutonnières might be deep purple ones.

Even though boutonnières are miniature in scale, there is plenty of scope for creativity by combining flowers, adding interesting foliage and using ribbon, braid, and pearl-headed pins to finish the arrangements. Another consideration is scent, since boutonnières are worn so close to the face.

**ABOVE** Three boutonnières from an English summer garden. From left, a tightly furled ruby red rose and an ivy leaf; sweetly scented white stock and a variegated ivy leaf; dainty pink spray roses with their own leaves.

**BELOW** White heather (which represents good luck) and a white rosebud make a delicate partnership, bound with lustrous velvet ribbon.

# There is scope for creativity by combining flowers and adding interesting foliage.

**RIGHT** These scented sweet peas have been given bead "stamens" and their stems bound with purple sequin trim.

**FAR RIGHT** Wedding flowers needn't be exotic or unusual. This delicate boutonnière uses a spray of viburnum, found in many gardens.

**BELOW RIGHT** A highly elegant and unusual boutonnière of orchids, miniature irises, and mimosa. The stem has been bound with ribbon in a distinctive criss-cross pattern.

**BELOW LEFT** These two boutonnières show how humble garden flowers—forget-me-nots—can be turned into pretty accessories. In the first, they offset a just-opened white rose, and in the second, they are framed by skimmia leaves. In both cases, narrow green ribbon provides the finishing touch.

**LEFT** Fine navy blue ribbon binds this boutonnière of grape hyacinths surrounded by a ruff of galax leaves.

**CENTER LEFT** Roses are a classic choice for boutonnières. Here, the perfect form of a white rose (you could also try a gardenia or camellia) is emphasized by a collar of dark galax leaves.

**BELOW LEFT** This ranunculus and feverfew boutonnière is fresh and natural—perfect for a relaxed country wedding.

**RIGHT** A head of green-tinged white hydrangea makes a pretty wrist corsage sewn onto pink and green braid.

**BELOW** This sequined bag makes a glamorous alternative to a traditional corsage and would make a statement at an evening reception. Three tiny posies of bicolored winter pansies in deep purple and yellow have been tucked into the bag and secured to the straps. Find pansies and violas at garden centers; you could also try spray roses.

Hyacinths, stephanotis, sweet peas, and stocks are just some of the many flowers with particularly glorious perfumes.

Corsages may be worn by the mothers, grandmothers, and sisters of the bride and groom. They're often pinned close to the neckline, so it's important that they're lightweight, to avoid any danger of tearing delicate dress fabrics. Wearing flowers on the wrist or tucking them into a tiny, ornate bag are stylish alternatives, giving a modern twist to a traditional idea.

ABOVE LEFT  All these boutonnières contain roses, although the two at the top look like something more exotic. For these, Martinique roses were turned inside out and wrapped in galax leaves. For the version below, a Grand Prix rose was arranged with winter jasmine and rose leaves.

ABOVE RIGHT  A row of immaculate pinkish-red rose and ivy leaf boutonnières. Roses are a wedding classic because of their associations with love, but they also last well when cut and come in a huge range of beautiful colors.

Wearing flowers on the wrist gives a modern twist to a traditional idea.

OPPOSITE, FROM TOP LEFT This golden yellow Illios rose glows against its ruff of variegated pittosporum leaves. An unfurled pink and green parrot tulip, accompanied by one of its slender leaves, heralds the arrival of spring. This Naranja rose nestling in ruffled burnt-orange cockscomb makes a strong impression.

OPPOSITE, BELOW There's no reason why boutonnières need all be the same. Here, complementary arrangements in soft, romantic colors are arranged on an ornate tray, ready to be picked up by the men of the bridal party. The plants include roses, snowberries, tulips, pittosporum leaves, and mimosa.

TOP This Candy Bianca rose, set in ivy, has exquisite shading from deepest pink to white. The stem is decorated with the finest of braids, trimmed with minute rosebuds, a beautiful detail which may be lost on guests but can be appreciated at close quarters by the wearer.

ABOVE In place of a posy, this bridesmaid sports a wrist corsage. The wedding scheme is modern and simple, with all-white flowers and dresses. Eucharis lilies are the key flower, chosen for their delicacy and exoticism. Their glamour helps the floral decorations to look contemporary, but unmistakably bridal. For the corsage, flower heads were attached to lengths of white satin ribbon with pearl-headed pins.

ABOVE Although a boutonnière is designed to be seen, the pleasure of wearing it can be increased if it has a delicious scent, too. Hyacinths exude a particularly powerful scent, and here flowerets from an ice-blue variety have been bound with narrow navy ribbon and secured with a pearl-headed pin.

# classic boutonnière

Traditional wedding attire for the groom
is a fairly sober affair, and a boutonnière
is an easy way to add a dash of color and
decoration to the ensemble. Roses are
the classic wedding flower. This stylishly
simple boutonnière uses a zingy orange
variety, elegantly accompanied by glossy
camellia leaves, but the design would
work just as well with any color of rose,
from white to black-red. Making the
boutonnière involves wiring the flower
and leaves, so it would be wise to have
a couple of practice runs before the day.

### FLOWERS & MATERIALS
*2 camellia leaves*
*1 orange Akito rose*

*scissors*
*thin wires*
*gutta tape*
*thick wires*

1 Cut the camellia stems to leave a short node. Take a thin wire, about 5½ in (14 cm) long, and fold in half. Insert the wire into a leaf as shown and pull through to the back. A flat loop will be visible at the front. Repeat for the second leaf.

2 Bend both wires flat against the back of the leaf. Leave the right wire straight and loop the left over the right, around the node, three times. Pull the wound wire straight and tape both together with gutta tape. Repeat for the second leaf.

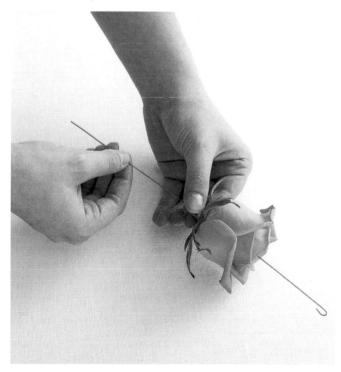

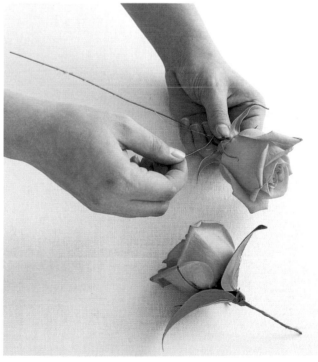

3 Cut the rose, leaving a 1 in (2 cm) stem. Insert a thick wire straight through the stem to emerge in the middle of the rose. Make a small loop at the top and pull the wire gently down so it feels secure and is buried in the flower head.

4 Place a thin wire crosswise behind the thick wire. Pull one side down and wrap the other end around it three times. Place a leaf on each side of the rose, fan out nicely, and tape leaves and rose in position. Cut wires 2 in (5 cm) long.

# PROJECT 12
# exotic boutonnière

It's easy to see why calla lilies are so popular with florists. There's the elegant shape, the soft gleam of the petals, and the fabulous colors—including white, burnt orange, burgundy, and pink—and they last well when cut. Their fluted silhouette suits long, columnar wedding dresses, but they also make striking boutonnières. Here, a burgundy calla is given minimal embellishment so as not to detract from its beauty. The loops of bear grass echo the curves of the petals, and a single bead gives a touch of sparkle.

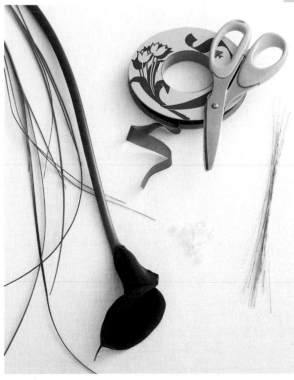

**FLOWERS & MATERIALS**
*bear grass*
*1 burgundy calla lily*

*thin wires*
*gutta tape*
*clear glass beads*
*scissors*

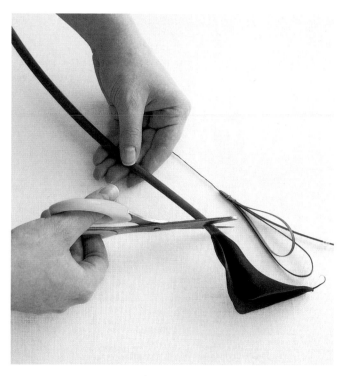

1  Take three strands of bear grass. Loop two over at different heights and leave one straight. Wire them together (see step 4, page 69) and tape the wire with gutta tape. Thread a bead onto the straight piece of bear grass.

2  Cut the lily stem short (because it is fleshy, you cannot wrap wire around it). When finished, the lily head should be nicely framed by the bear grass, with all the elements showing. The top of the lily can bruise, so try not to handle it too much.

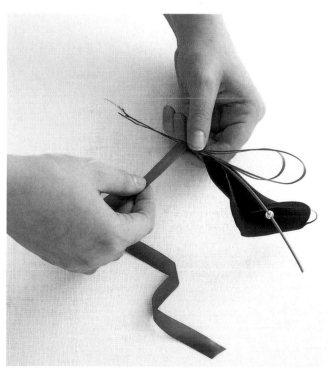

3  Insert a wire horizontally through the lily stem. Pull the ends down. Wrap one wire around the other (not around the stem). Tape over the wire. If you have a lily with a thick stem you could wire it like the rose in steps 3 and 4, page 69.

4  Shape the boutonnière as required and tape the bear grass and lily together, also taping the wires. Trim to 2 in (5 cm). Take out of water two hours before needed and dry on paper towels, as the lily stem will leak sap and color.

# PROJECT 13
# classic corsage

Opportunities to wear or carry flowers are few and far between, so it's nice for the mothers (and, perhaps, grandmothers and sisters) of the bride and groom to be able to wear the feminine equivalent of the boutonnière, a corsage. The traditional corsage—a miniature posy attached to the collar, lapel, or bodice of an outfit—is less popular than it once was. It's a pity because, as this elegant arrangement of white freesias, berries, roses, and jasmine shows, there need be nothing old-fashioned or fussy about a classic corsage. The flowers are wired to keep the arrangement extra-light, and it is attached by a concealed magnet, to save wear on fine fabrics. For those who like flowers displayed in a more modern way, there's the option of a wrist corsage (see project 14).

**FLOWERS & MATERIALS**
*spray of white freesia*
*spray of white hypericum berries*
*1 white Akito rose*
*1 large ivy leaf*
*spray of jasmine*

*scissors*
*thin wires*
*gutta tape*
*thick wires*
*corsage magnet*

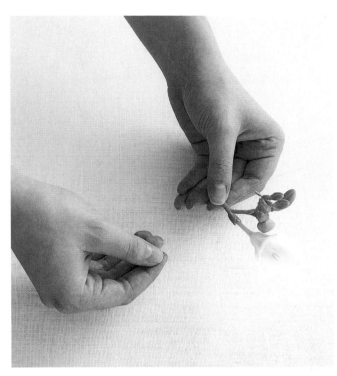

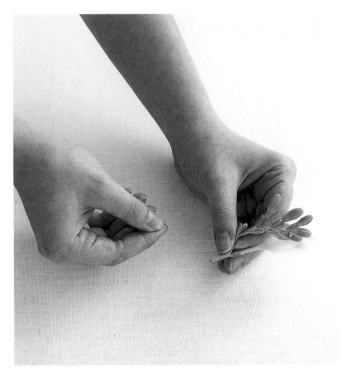

1 Cut a freesia flower head, leaving a 1 in (2 cm) stalk. Insert a thin wire horizontally through the stalk. Creating a wire stem will make the flower stronger and means its position within the corsage can be adjusted.

2 Bring one wire straight down, following the line of the freesia stalk, and wind the other wire around it three times. (This method of wiring is called a single-leg mount.) Secure with gutta tape.

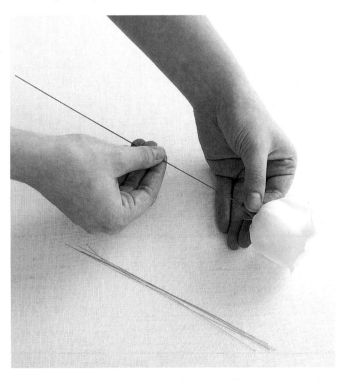

3 Cut one small side shoot and the main top shoot from the spray of hypericum. Wire and tape both pieces, as you did the freesia. Having two pieces gives you the flexibility to create a good shape for the corsage.

4 Cut the rose head, leaving a short stem. Wire the rose using the method shown for the classic boutonnière (see steps 3 and 4, page 69). Insert a thick wire through the center, then strengthen it with a thin horizontal wire.

5　Take a thin wire, about 5½ in (14 cm) long, and fold in half. Insert the wire no more than halfway up the ivy leaf and pull through to the back. A flat loop will be visible at the front. Make sure the wire is at the mid-point of the leaf's width.

6　Bend both wires flat against the back of the leaf. Leave the right wire straight and loop the left over the right three times. Pull the wound wire straight and tape both together with gutta tape. Take the tape down to cover the wire.

7　Tape the freesia together with a spray of jasmine, as shown. Tape the hypericum sprigs on each side of the rose and arrange attractively. Place the two flower bunches together, with the rose and freesia at the same height.

8　Place the flowers onto the ivy leaf and tape all the stems together. Trim stems to 2½ in (6 cm) long. Tape the thinner part of the magnet to the back of the corsage, at the top of the ivy stem, ready to be attached to the wearer's dress.

# PROJECT 14
## wrist corsage

This stylish and fun wrist corsage might appeal to bridesmaids as well as female relatives of the bride and groom. Despite the exoticism of cymbidium orchids, they are a practical choice, too. Orchids last well when cut and have such striking flowers that just one makes a strong statement, making them cost-effective. You could try other varieties, such as moth or Singapore orchids. The bloom must be firmly attached to the ribbon so it doesn't fall off when the wearer uses her hands, so a hot glue gun is necessary.

### FLOWERS & MATERIALS
*spray of lime-green cymbidium orchid*

*white ribbon (ours was 1³/₄ in, 4 cm wide)*
*scissors*
*pen*
*hot glue gun and glue stick*

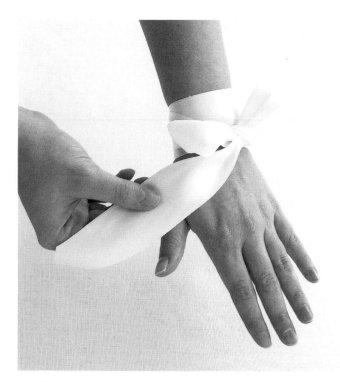

1 Wrap ribbon around the bridesmaid's wrist to determine its length. The ribbon should wind around the wrist once and overlap, making a neat bow on top of the wrist. Leave a little extra ribbon for working and cut the ends off at a slant.

2 Cut a flower bud from the orchid stem with as short a stalk as possible (be careful not to damage the flower head). Mark the center of the ribbon's length with a pen. If your ribbon is crumpled, iron it with a cool iron at this point.

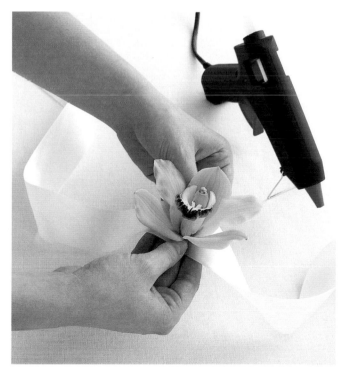

3 Heat the glue gun and place a dab of glue onto the back of the orchid stalk and part of the flower. Glue the orchid to the pen mark on the ribbon. If you have not used a glue gun before, practice on something soft first, such as fabric.

4 Let the glue dry. The corsage is now ready to tie to the wearer's wrist. Do this as near to the ceremony as possible. Tie fairly securely just above the wrist, so the corsage doesn't get in the way while eating and drinking.

# Flowers for the reception

A wedding is a celebration of love. The right flowers will conjure up a romantic, joyful atmosphere, bringing beauty, color, and scent to a reception. Position large displays carefully where they'll have the maximum impact, then use smaller arrangements and thoughtfully chosen floral details—single blooms placed on plates, sprigs tucked into napkins or sitting atop boxes of favors, and posies attached to chair backs—to tie everything together.

LEFT AND BELOW  With its gilded overmantel mirror, the fireplace in this room is a focal point and merits an impressive floral display—an elegant swag, held in place by two large clusters of flowers. The reception color scheme, a classic combination of white, cream, and golden yellow in the form of roses, tulips, snowberries, mimosa, and ivy, complements the room.

OPPOSITE ABOVE  Cream spray roses in a silver pot show how elegant simplicity can be.

# creating a scheme

Of all the decorative tools at your disposal, flowers are by far the most effective when it comes to customizing and personalizing a space such as a hotel banquet hall or tent, creating a welcoming and celebratory atmosphere. It's natural for the reception flowers to be inspired by the bride and bridesmaids' bouquets, but there's scope to use a greater range of flowers and even colors, too, creating variations on the theme.

Begin by choosing positions for the floral displays within the space. To make the most of your budget, target areas for your biggest arrangements that are obvious focal points: for instance, entrances and exits;

**ABOVE LEFT** White and green is soft and romantic. The clear glass vase brims with calla lilies, snowberries, lady's mantle, eucharis lilies, stocks, and hydrangeas.

**ABOVE CENTER** At this informal country wedding, galvanized buckets overflow with garden plants, including crab apples, roses, and snowberries.

**ABOVE RIGHT** A polished silver dish holds an elegant table decoration of roses, tulips, stocks, snowberries, and mimosa, in shades of cream and gold.

ABOVE This simple but dramatic avenue of single rosebuds in small glass vases shows what can be done even on a limited budget.

LEFT A display at the entrance to the reception—here, a loose arrangement of garden foliage with crab apples, feverfew, and lilies—sets the tone.

BELOW This scented lily of the valley in a white-painted terracotta pot is a place-card holder, flower arrangement, and favor all in one.

the place where the receiving line will be; fireplaces, alcoves, niches, or windowsills. Then think about centerpieces and floral details for the tables. It's nice if the bride's table, at least, has a striking centerpiece, or even a swag along its length if it's long and faces the rest of the room. If the other tables are round, a central display (one large arrangement or a cluster of smaller ones) works well; if guests are seated at long trestle tables, a series of arrangements down their length looks good. Whatever you choose, don't let the centerpieces get too tall, or they will impede rather than encourage conversation between guests.

BELOW A huge weeping willow in a country garden is the setting for a relaxed outdoor reception that celebrates summer. The long trestle tables, draped with white cotton sheets, are punctuated by tall glass vases overflowing with cottage-garden flowers, among them lupines, roses, sweet peas, stocks, Queen Anne's lace, and ripening blackberries. Deep pinkish-red shades are used alongside the whites, greens, and pale pinks, to add richness to the color scheme.

# Arrangements down the length of long trestle tables look good.

**RIGHT** Strategic use of a single accent color gives this table setting a stylish, cohesive look. For the centerpiece, deep pinkish-red roses and white stephanotis sit in a pewter dish. Rose heads of the same color sit at each place, their color echoed by the plates, glassware, and candles.

**CENTER RIGHT** This posy of roses, freesias, veronica, crab apples, feverfew, and garden foliage, hung over a bench with ribbon, anchors one end of a jasmine swag.

**BELOW LEFT** A lusciously dark chocolate wedding cake, covered in chocolate frills, has been studded with jewel-bright poppy anemones and velvety gray-green stachys leaves, which stand out vividly against the dark background.

**BELOW RIGHT** A fresh pink rosebud, its petals intricately curled, tops a favor box.

Then think about smaller floral details. You could decorate each guest's place setting with a single, gorgeous bloom— such as a rose, camellia, or orchid—on the plate or in the glass. Instead of place cards, you could plant miniature terracotta pots (left plain or painted) with growing flowers such as violas, lily of the valley, or alyssum, and tie a name label to the pot with narrow ribbon. If you're organizing a spring wedding, you could plant bulbs well ahead so that they'll be in bloom for the wedding. These could also double as favors for guests to take home at the end of the reception. Napkins can be secured

**ABOVE RIGHT** For this chair-back display, a twig circlet has been embellished with ivy and shocking pink poppy anemones, then firmly tied on with matching pink ribbon.

**RIGHT** Fresh petals make romantic (and biodegradable) confetti. Rose petals have a lovely texture and come in many colors. More garden roses are scented than cultivated ones.

with sprigs of flowers and ribbon or cord, and posies or wreaths can be fixed to chair backs and decorated with ribbon. Scatter the tables with fresh rose petals or add shallow bowls, filled with water, floating candles, and flower heads. Even the cake can be embellished with tiny posies of flowers, an easier and cheaper option than iced decorations. And, to complete the floral theme, why not send guests home with pastel-colored envelopes filled with easy-to-grow seeds such as poppies, or little fabric bags containing spring or summer bulbs?

RIGHT A single, full-blown rose next to a beribboned box of favors turns this place setting into an elegant still-life.

CENTER RIGHT Use fresh flowers and foliage to bring the garden indoors and create instantly pretty details. Here, a pleated napkin has been cinched with

a stem of variegated euonymus foliage and Queen Anne's lace.

FAR RIGHT Posies of ice-cream pink hydrangeas, scented stephanotis, and snowberries decorate each tier of this cake. The lacy delicacy of the flowers complements the icing pearls that define each layer.

ABOVE LEFT Fresh flowers are not a must at the table. These silk cabbage roses, complete with buds and leaves, look just about as good as the real thing and are guaranteed not to wilt on the hottest of days. At each place setting, they double as favors to be taken home by the guests.

ABOVE RIGHT A chair-back posy of deep yellow roses, tulips, and snowberries, tied with white satin ribbon, complements a gilt chair elegantly. Rather than having place cards on the table, a name card has been attached to the posy, meaning guests will have to stop and admire the flowers.

**LEFT AND ABOVE** Using fresh flowers is a quick and easy way to embellish a simply iced cake and turn it into something spectacular. Make sure that the flowers you use have not been sprayed with any garden chemicals and are edible. Here, aromatic lavender, deep red roses, and pink-to-white spray roses look and smell romantic and summery.

# long centerpiece

This arrangement is designed for a long rectangular table rather than a round one and would make a spectacular addition to the bride's table. The container needn't be particularly decorative, since it will be obscured by the flowers and foliage. The aromatic eucalyptus with its small, globular leaves, the long, thin blades of bear grass, and the elegant spires of lysimachia give the arrangement an airy quality and frame the blowsy softness of the flowers at the center of the display. The mixture of gray-green, white, cream, and lime green is beautifully fresh and calm. It's versatile, too, suiting almost any style of wedding and any time of year. If the oasis is kept moist, the centerpiece should keep its looks for four or five days, so let someone take it home after the reception.

**FLOWERS & MATERIALS**

*about 4 stems eucalyptus*
*4 large cream Vendella roses*
*2 white Akito roses*
*6 lime-green carnations*
*about 3 stems green hypericum berries*
*10 white lysimachias*
*4 stems cream spray roses*
*bear grass*

*oasis block and dish*
*knife*
*oasis tape*
*scissors*
*water spray*

1 Cut the oasis block to fit the holder. We used half a block, about 4½ x 3 in (11 x 7 cm) and 3 in (8 cm) high. Strip the lower leaves of the eucalyptus and cut the ends at a slant. Reserve some long pieces with pointed ends.

2 Soak the oasis block in cold water for one minute. Place in the oasis dish and secure with oasis tape, as shown. Don't use any more tape than this, because you need maximum space for inserting flowers and foliage.

3 Insert a long stem of eucalyptus about ½ in (1 cm) into the center of each end of the oasis. These will determine the finished length of the piece and should be about twice the length of the oasis block. Add two more stems at each end.

4 Start filling in the sides of the oasis. The foliage should be about half the length of the pieces used on the ends. Aim to create a rounded shape to the sides. Now add short foliage pieces to the top, including a taller piece in the center.

5   Insert a large Vendella rose in the center. The head should be about 3 in (8 cm) above the oasis. Place an Akito rose and a Vendella rose in opposite corners and use the remaining Vendella rose to fill the center.

6   Insert three carnations in the remaining opposite corners. The top of the oasis should be getting full. Use hypericum sprigs to fill gaps. Aim for a rounded shape, decreasing in height toward the ends.

7   Add the lysimachia stems to give soft, flowing edges to the design. Fill in any remaining gaps with the smaller spray rose heads. You can also use any unopened rosebuds on the sprays to fill in small gaps.

8   Bunch three or four stems of bear grass (trim the ends at a slant). Insert at one corner, on the top of the oasis. The ends should droop down and spray out. Insert five or six bunches like this. Spray the arrangement with water to keep it fresh.

# contemporary centerpiece

This cool, modern arrangement is all about unusual shapes, textures, and plant combinations, mixing the familiar and the exotic. The cream roses anchor it firmly in the bridal realm, while the anthuriums, or painter's palettes, with their extraordinary, almost reflective petals, introduce tropical lushness. The limes add zesty color (matched almost exactly by the feathery chrysanthemums), another tropical element that also makes the centerpiece appropriately mouthwatering. With so many intriguing and contrasting textures, it's also important to include a few touches of darker or brighter color. The painter's palette spikes and the dark stripes of the variegated foliage provide interest, while not detracting from the overall softness of the color scheme.

### FLOWERS & MATERIALS
*2 limes*
*2 green shamrock chrysanthemums*
*8 cream roses*
*3 white anthuriums*
*3 green anthuriums*
*variegated foliage such as lime tips*

*knife*
*petroleum jelly*
*cocktail sticks*
*oasis block*
*square vase or container, preferably reflective*
*(Note: this will show, so it*
*needs to be good-looking)*
*oasis tape*
*scissors*

1 Cut the limes in half and coat the cut sides with petroleum jelly. This will stop them from discoloring. Insert a cocktail stick into the pointed end of each half. Go about halfway in; you don't want the stick to pierce the other side.

2 Cut the oasis block to fit inside your container, but make it slightly taller than the container. Soak the oasis block and replace it in the container. Use oasis tape to secure it, as shown. Keep the ends quite short, so they won't show.

3 Place the two shamrock chrysanthemums in the center of the oasis. (If yours have particularly large flowers, you may only need to use one.) They should sit about 3 in (8 cm) above the surface, and will be the design's highest point.

4 Insert the limes at three corners of the oasis. Put two halves in one corner and one each in two others, leaving one corner empty (this design is deliberately asymmetrical). They should sit at an angle, as shown, rather than upright.

5 Cut the rose stems to give a pointed tip. Leave 2½ in (6 cm) of stem. Insert two groups of three roses and one pair, to fill space between the limes. Insert the roses at an angle so the heads face down, for an overflowing feel to the design.

6 Use the anthuriums to fill in gaps on the top and at the sides of the arrangement. Insert the white ones first. As they are such striking flowers, it's a good idea to experiment with a few locations before pushing them in firmly.

7 If necessary, you can reposition the anthuriums in the oasis, as there is still foliage to add. Once you are happy with the white flowers, add the green anthuriums. The container is filling up now, so take care not to squash the roses.

8 Cut the top tips from the foliage, as shown. Insert the foliage to fill any gaps, with some draping over the edges (remember to cover any visible oasis tape). Fold back some of the leaves to give a rolled effect—this looks good on top.

# traditional centerpiece

Rings have been symbols of everlasting love for thousands of years, and a circular
table arrangement echoes this nicely. The secret of this display's success is that
it uses enough plant material to give a really full and luscious effect. The hydrangea
heads are a key ingredient here; their lacy, domed heads fill out the display, giving it
a soft, blowsy quality, while the large roses also help to create an overflowing look.
Freesias (which contribute scent) and lisianthus fill in any gaps prettily, and narrow
spires of veronica add vertical accents in contrast to the soft roundedness of the
centerpiece. Candles are popular at weddings for their mellow, romantic light.
The chunky cream candle is a strong focal point, and as evening approaches,
it will bathe the table in a warm glow.

### FLOWERS & MATERIALS
*large bunch salal foliage*
*1 or 2 mixed hydrangea heads (enough to give 5 pieces)*
*6 pink-and-white Dolce Vita roses*
*20 white freesias*
*5 white double lisianthus*
*8 stems purple veronica*

*oasis ring 12 in (30 cm) in diameter, in a holder*
*scissors*
*pillar candle*

1  Soak the oasis ring for one minute. Cut the salal into stems about 3 in (8 cm), each with about four leaves. Insert around the outside edge of the ring, at an angle so the leaves slant downward. Add a layer near the bottom and near the top.

2  Using bunches of smaller leaves, add foliage to the inside of the ring to cover the oasis and holder. Don't overfill, as some of the flowers you add later will take up space in the center, and you will need room to add the candle.

3  Cut the bloom from a stem or two of hydrangea, then cut the heads to give you five pieces, each with a short stem of about 2 in (4 cm). Don't worry if they are not exactly the same size. Insert them on top of the ring at regular intervals.

4  Cut the rose stems to about 3 in (8 cm). Add them in pairs between the hydrangea heads, as shown. Our roses were a large variety; if you use smaller roses, you may need to allow three to a group.

5 Cut the freesia flower heads, leaving a 2 in (5 cm) stem. Insert on top of the ring, first filling the gaps between hydrangea pieces where there are no roses. Add more freesias at the top outer edge of the ring, to hang down.

6 Cut the lisianthus, leaving slightly longer stems than you did for the freesias. Use these to fill the sides of the ring, as shown. Make sure the heads are visible between the foliage. Use any spare lisianthus to fill gaps on top.

7 Add the veronica stems to soften the edges of the arrangement, both inside and outside the ring. Check for any gaps and areas of visible oasis and fill them with salal leaves (remember the ring will be viewed from close up).

8 Add the candle. Our candle was about 8 in (20 cm) tall. If your candle is not tall enough, place something firm, such as the lid from a coffee jar, underneath. As a variation, try some single-color roses in place of the bicolored ones here.

# PROJECT 18
## floral napkin holder

White china and clear glass are the norm at many reception venues, and white is also the classic option for table linen. These neutral elements need enlivening if they aren't to appear bland, and floral details are one of the best ways of personalizing a table setting. These napkin holders use a gentle palette of green, white, and pink. All the flowers are small and delicate, and their contrasting shapes create an interesting still-life, while the lustrous velvet ribbon contrasts attractively with the plain linen napkin.

### FLOWERS & MATERIALS
*1 stem pink veronica*
*1 white freesia*
*1 stem green skimmia*

*scissors*
*thin wire*
*white gutta tape*
*narrow velvet ribbon*

1  Cut the veronica, freesia, and skimmia to leave a short stem, with any lower leaves removed. Pierce the stem of each element (above, the skimmia) horizontally with thin wire.

2  Pull one end of the wire straight down against the stem. Wrap the other wire around the straight wire and the stem three times. Repeat for all three elements.

3  Cover all the wires with white gutta tape to blend with a white napkin. Arrange the three flowers together, with the veronica highest and in the center, and tape them together.

4  Cut the wire ends off neatly. Place the flowers on a folded napkin. Keeping the ribbon flat, wind it around the napkin. Tie the ribbon to hide the join of the taped wires.

# chair-back decoration

Decorating the back of each chair at the bride's table, or the bride and groom's chairs, is a nice touch. This display is a generous size, but could be scaled down, and it can also decorate the front of the table or a seating-planboard. Large-leafed foliage creates a full shape and a backdrop for the flowers. The bold lilies are balanced by the airy jasmine and the soft moluccella (bells of Ireland). The roses provide shots of brilliance against the cooler shades, but could be replaced by a softer shade for a different look.

### FLOWERS & MATERIALS
*salal stems*
*1 or 2 lilies, depending on size*
*2 stems moluccella*
*3 long-stemmed orange roses*
*jasmine*

*green twine*
*scissors*
*wide ribbon*

1 Make a backing frame for the design with salal foliage. Aim for a fan shape—a long piece framed by pieces each side. Our longest piece was 14 in (35 cm). When you are happy with the shape, tie the stems with green twine.

2 Add a lily stem, with an open flower and a few buds, on top of the salal leaves, in the center. Use a second, if needed. Frame it with a stem of moluccella on either side, as shown. These additions should sit flat without needing to be tied in.

3 Place the roses where they will be seen (remember the arrangement will hang down). Try varying the lengths of the stems. Add jasmine to the sides and center, to trail softly around the other flowers. Tie all together with twine.

4 Trim all the stems neatly and tie the arrangement securely to its chair. (You could use wire if it is difficult to secure.) Wrap ribbon around the twine, to cover the mechanics, then finish with a large bow, leaving trailing ends.

# PROJECT 20
## cake topper

Making sugar-paste decorations is a
time-consuming and skilled job, but
using fresh flowers to turn a plain,
white-iced cake into a work of art is
simplicity itself. Bouvardia is ideal
because of the delicacy of its flowers
and the ease with which small sprigs
can be bunched together, and the green
hypericum berries are like glossy beads.
The flowers must be completely dry
before they come into contact with the
cake. Make sure the pins are safely
removed before the cake is cut up.

**FLOWERS & MATERIALS**

*hypericum berries*
*bouvardia sprigs*

*white gutta tape*
*scissors*
*pearl-headed pins*

1  Cut one sprig of hypericum berries and two of bouvardia flowers for each tier of the cake. Bunch them together, with the hypericum sprig between the bouvardias.

2  Tape the stalks together very neatly using white gutta tape, which will not show against the white cake icing. Take the tape to the end of the stalks and trim the ends neatly.

3  Push a pearl-headed pin through each bunch, as shown, and insert into the boards on which each layer of cake sits. Stagger the position of the bunches as they go up the cake.

4  Cut more sprigs of bouvardia flowers and arrange them on top of the cake. Cut them quite short and they will pile up to form a rounded dome shape.

# working with flowers

• If you're buying flowers a couple of days before the wedding, get them in bud so they'll be open in time for the big day. If you buy flowers already in full bloom, make sure you can arrange them quickly while they're still perfect.

• Don't be afraid to ask a florist for advice when buying flowers. They should be knowledgeable about their stock and able to answer any questions you have.

• Check the quality of what you buy. Look for healthy foliage, strong stems, and undamaged buds and flowers.

• If you're using flowers from your own garden, they may not last as long as commercially grown flowers. Garden flowers, like purchased flowers, should stand in fresh water before use.

• If you're producing a lot of arrangements, figure out exactly what you'll need on paper, and allow time for a trial run if you think you need it.

• Always buy more stems than is specified in our projects—to allow for flowers getting damaged or broken, or being less than perfect.

- Look for bright yellow stamens when buying lilies; old lilies (of all varieties) have dark stamens.

- Make sure that any containers used for soaking flowers are clean and bacteria-free. Rinse them with water containing a little bleach before using.

- Give flowers a long drink (ideally, a day) in cool water before you arrange them.

- A commercial flower food will prolong the life of cut flowers. Sugar, lemonade, or aspirin added to the water will also keep flowers healthier for longer.

- If you use carnations, cut just above a leaf nodule before putting them in water.

- Soak oasis for a minute; oversoaking makes it fragile and unusable. Inserting too many flowers will also eventually cause the oasis to crumble.

- Before arranging flowers, carefully strip the stems of thorns and leaves using a sharp knife. A quick alternative is to wear heavy gardening gloves and run your thumb and finger down the stem. When planning, allow for the length of time it will take you to prepare the plant material, particularly if there's a lot of it.

- Rose stems should be cut at an angle to aid water uptake. Soft-stemmed flowers (such as tulips, hyacinths, and calla lilies) can be cut on the straight and should be placed in a container only a quarter full of water, to keep stems from becoming waterlogged and soggy.

- Remove lily stamens; their pollen stains anything it touches bright orange.

- Gutta tape is stretchy. To make it thinner, pull it out as you use it.

- Cut stems with a knife at an angle to make them easier to push into oasis. If you make a mistake when positioning a flower in oasis, fill in the hole with a snippet of stem. If oasis is too full of holes, it can start to collapse.

- Spray table arrangements with water to keep them fresh and the oasis moist.

- Keep all finished arrangements somewhere cool and dark, but don't be tempted to store any flowers, including boutonnières and corsages, in the fridge.

- The length of a teardrop bouquet should be tailored to the height of the bride: the taller the bride, the longer the bouquet can be. For a petite bride, a tied bunch is probably more flattering.

- For pinning boutonnières to lapels, buy pearl-headed pins, which look more special than normal dressmaking pins.

- Some of the longest-lasting flowers are chrysanthemums, carnations, hydrangeas, roses, and calla lilies. Sweet peas and poppy anemones, though beautiful, have a short life once cut.

- Calla lilies have a long cut life—about three weeks in a vase. The stems retain a lot of water and tend to leak, so take them out of water a few hours before needed and wipe the stems again just before the ceremony. For the same reason, if you are binding a lily bouquet such as the one on page 28, don't take the ribbon all the way to the end.

- Prices of exotic flowers such as callas and orchids can rise markedly during the peak wedding months (May to July), or if supplies are low. If you're on a budget, go for flowers less prone to fluctuations in price, such as roses and carnations.

# flower directory

**ANTHURIUM (Painter's palette)**
Impressive sculptural blooms that bruise easily. Stems are usually supplied with a plastic cover; keep this on until needed.

**ASPARAGUS FERN**
(*Asparagus densiflorus*)
An exceptionally delicate and feathery fern, suitable for romantic arrangements.

**ASPIDISTRA (*Aspidistra*)**
Large, smooth, glossy dark green leaves that can make a bouquet "collar."

**BACHELOR'S BUTTONS**
(*Centaurea cyanus*)
A true blue flower, rare in the flower world.

**BEAR GRASS**
Strikingly architectural and contemporary foliage with useful bladelike leaves.

**BOUVARDIA (*Bouvardia*)**
An excellent bridal flower available in pinks, mauves, and whites.

**CALLA LILY (*Zantedeschia aethiopica*)**
Dramatic, sculptural blooms; expensive in the summer months.

**CAMELLIA (*Camellia*)**
Flowers are white, pink, or red, and the leaves are dark, glossy, and very attractive. Useful for winter weddings as an alternative to roses.

**CARNATION (*Dianthus*)**
Long-lasting, excellent value, and available in a huge color range. Popular for boutonnières. Also known as pinks.

**CHRYSANTHEMUM (*Chrysanthemum*)**
Exceptionally long-lasting and very good value for money. Available in a variety of colors and forms, including the spidery shamrock chrysanthemum.

**EUCALYPTUS (*Eucalyptus*)**
Attractive foliage with small, aromatic, gray-green globular leaves.

**EUCHARIS LILY (*Eucharis*)**
Exceptionally elegant white flowers.

**EUONYMUS (*Euonymus*)**
Attractive foliage; the leaves can be variegated with white or gold and some varieties produce pink or red fall color.

**FORGET-ME-NOT (*Myosotis*)**
Unpretentious, very pretty blue and pink flowers. Gives prolific flowers all spring.

**FREESIA (*Freesia*)**
Good value scented flowers on arching stems, which can provide an extra shape to an arrangement. They come in many colors and are widely available.

**GALAX (*Galax*)**
Large, glossy green leaves.

**GINGER LILY (*Alpinia*)**
Tropical, colorful flowers. Expensive but striking and dramatic, they would be ideal for a non-traditional ceremony.

**GLORY LILY (*Gloriosa superba*)**
Exotic red blooms edged with gold.

**GRAPE HYACINTH (*Muscari*)**
Colors range from pale to deep blue. Useful for reception table pots and decorations.

**GUELDER ROSE (*Viburnum opulus*)**
A shrub with pompomlike white blooms.

**HELICONIA (*Heliconia*)**
Sculptural tropical blooms in spicy colors.

**HELLEBORE (*Helleborus*)**
Winter-flowering and so useful for winter weddings. Subtly beautiful flowers in greens, pinks to deep purple, and white.

**HOSTA (*Hosta*)**
Large, glossy leaves, often variegated. Useful for table arrangements.

**HYACINTH (*Hyacinthus*)**
Highly scented; useful for table decorations.

**HYDRANGEA (*Hydrangea*)**
Best purchased as whole plants—cut stems wilt immediately out of water. Useful for late summer and fall color, the huge flower heads come in white, pinks, and blues.

**HYPERICUM** (St. John's wort)
Green, orange, and cream berried foliage. Good for filling gaps in arrangements.

**ICELAND POPPY** (*Papaver croceum*)
Available in white, yellows, and burnt orange. Before using, condition the cut stems by singeing with a match.

**IRIS** (*Iris*)
Irises come in a huge color range, including white, yellow, blue, and purple.

**IVY** (*Hedera helix*)
Ivy is found in many gardens, but can also be purchased. Comes in many variegated forms as well as plain green.

**JASMINE** (*Jasminum*)
There are winter and summer jasmines; we used winter (*Jasminum nudiflorum*).

**LADY'S MANTLE** (*Alchemilla mollis*)
The frothy lime-green flowers are a very useful foil for other flower colors.

**LAVENDER** (*Lavandula*)
Best bought in plant form. Good for adding scent to a bouquet or table arrangement.

**LILY** (*Lilium*)
Spectacular large flowers that make a real impact in a bouquet, from white to deep pink. Many varieties are highly scented.

**LILY OF THE VALLEY**
(*Convallaria majalis*)
The delicate, scented flowers are best suited to a small posy or a table setting.

**LIME TIPS**
The striped variagated foliage used in the modern centerpiece.

**LISIANTHUS** (*Eustoma*)
The flowers, often in white, lilac, or pink, are reminiscent of roses. Good value and widely available.

**LUPINE** (*Lupinus*)
Tall and dramatic, in a wide color range.

**LYSIMACHIA** (*Lysimachia*)
These long, elegant tapered flowers are useful as vertical accents.

**MARGARITA**
(*Argyranthemum frutescens*)
Cheerful white daisylike flowers.

**MOLUCCELLA** (Bells of Ireland)
Tall stems of unusual green flowers.

**ORCHID**
This large family of flowers includes the varieties **Dendrobium** (Singapore orchids), **Cymbidium** and **Phalaenopsis** (moth orchids). They are expensive, but excellent wedding flowers: available in a wide choice of shades, long-lasting, and exquisite. Used sparingly, they will still make an impact.

**PEONY** (*Paeonia*)
Huge, blowsy flowers in colors from white to deep pink, sometimes scented.

**POPPY ANEMONE**
(*Anemone coronaria* De Caen)
Large, open flowers with bold black centers, in blue, pink, red, and white.

**QUEEN ANNE'S LACE**
(*Anthriscus sylvestris*)
Delicate white flowers found in country lanes, but also grown commercially.

**RANUNCULUS** (*Ranunculus*)
Beautiful, tightly furled flowers in an unusual color range.

**ROSE** (*Rosa*)
Commercially grown flowers are usually scentless. If you want scent, you will need to beg or borrow some garden varieties.

**Akito** (various colors) A very good all-round rose for wedding arrangements.

**Ballet** (cerise) Smaller than Akito.

**Black Baca** (deep red)
Expensive at Christmas and Valentine's.

**Dolce Vita** (white/cerise pink mix)
A bicolored rose with a large head.

**Eskimo** (small white)
Cheaper due to its smaller size.

**Grand Prix** (blood red)
The best red rose you can buy.

**Sweet Akito** (pink)
A very good all-round rose for weddings.

**Vendella** (cream)
A very good all-round rose for weddings.

**Vivianne** (spray white)
Sprays of smaller rose heads, useful for filling gaps and adding to corsages.

**RUSCUS** (*Ruscus*)
Comes in two lengths—the longer variety has smaller, finer leaves.

**SALAL**
Most of this useful dark green foliage comes from Florida.

**SCABIOUS** (*Scabiosa*)
Pretty summer flowers in pastel shades.

**SKIMMIA** (*Skimmia*)
A useful foliage shrub with dark green leaves and white flowers.

**SNAPDRAGON** (*Antirrhinum*)
Cottage-garden favorite in a very wide range of pretty, bright colors.

**STEPHANOTIS** (*Stephanotis floribunda*)
Exquisite white waxy flowers with a beautiful scent.

**STOCK** (*Matthiola*)
Pretty pastel flowers in white, pale pink, and lilac. Usually scented and good value.

**SUNFLOWER** (*Helianthus annuus*)
Large, cheerful yellow summer flowers.

**SWEET PEA** (*Lathyrus odoratus*)
Not very long-lasting, but beautiful flowers in a huge range of colors including white, purples, pinks, and sometimes red. Well known for their perfume, but commercially grown varieties are not always scented.

**TULIP** (*Tulipa*)
A huge range of colors and forms, including ruffled and striped varieties.

**VERONICA** (*Veronica*)
Elegant, tapering spires of flowers, usually in white, purple, or pink. Useful as a contrasting form to round flowers.

# sources

## ASSOCIATIONS

**American Institute of Floral Designers**
410-752-3318
www.aifd.org
Offers directory of more than 1,200
certified floral designers nationwide.

**California Cut Flowers Commission**
831-728-7333
www.ccfc.org
Nonprofit organization offers information
on wedding flowers, and designing
bouquets, garlands, and centerpieces.

**International Flower Picture Database**
www.flowerweb.com
In-depth resource for floral designers,
novice and otherwise.

**International Cut Flower Growers
Association**
www.rosesinc.org
Provides helpful information on selecting
and caring for cut flowers.

**Society of American Florists**
800-336-4743
www.aboutflowers.com
Consumer information from the national
trade association for the floral industry.
Helpful facts about flower varieties, color
trends, the care of cut flowers, and more.

## CRAFT SUPPLIES AND VASES

The following supply the materials and
tools needed to make the projects in this
book; everything from glue guns, gutta
tape, and stub wire to small gift bags.

**Bridallink Store**
www.bridallink.com
This "everything bridal" store is where
to go when you need corsage magnets,
ready-made bouquet holders, or other
hard-to-track down floral supplies.

**www.eBay.com**
Consider this reliable source for any
supplies or embellishments you have
trouble tracking down in retail stores.

**Crate and Barrel**
650 Madison Avenue
New York, NY 10022
212-308-0011
www.crateandbarrel.com
Vases and containers. Visit the website
to find a store near you.

**Hobby Lobby**
405-745-1100
www.hobbylobby.com
Order online from this all-around craft
store, or find a retail outlet near you.

**Michael's**
800-Michaels
www.michaels.com
One-stop shopping for crafting needs.

**Oriental Trading Company, Inc.**
800-875-8480
www.orientaltrading.com
Everything from crafting tools to party
supplies can be found at this vibrant
online retailer and catalog.

Pearl Paint
308 Canal Street
New York, NY 10013
800-221-6845 x2297
www.pearlpaint.com
This art-supply store also supplies floral
designers with tools and embellishments.

Save-On-Crafts
831-768-8428
www.safe-on-crafts.com
Shop here for 20 to 50% off floral
supplies and wedding necessities.

Staples
800-3STAPLE
www.staples.com
Crafting supplies at reasonable prices.

WireStore
888-773-8769
www.wirestore.com
Wide selection of wire frames for
bouquets and other floral arrangements.

## BOUQUET EMBELLISHMENTS
## (BEADS, RIBBONS, AND MORE)

Bead Works
23 Church Street
Cambridge, MA 02138
617-868-9777
www.beadworks.com
From delicate seed beads to decadent
semi-precious stone beads.

Calico Corners
800-213-6366
www.calico corners.com
Over 100 retail outlets offer a wide
range of fabrics, buttons, and trims.

COD Wholesale
888-345-0418
www.codwholesale.com
Wholesalers of ribbons, tulle, organza,
and many other bouquet necessities.

JoAnn Fabrics & Crafts
800-525-4951
www.joann.com
Ribbons, tulle, and other bouquet-
appropriate items, online and in stores.

Renaissance Ribbons
P.O. Box 699
Oregon House, CA 95962
530-692-0842
www.renaissanceribbons.com
Trims, ribbons, and other notions.

## CANDLES (DISCOUNT/BULK)

Bridal Shop
941-475-0888
www.bridalshopstore.com
Bridal supplies, including wedding-
appropriate candles and candle holders.

GenWax
800-WAX-STOR
www.genwax.com
Scented and unscented candles in a
wide variety of shapes, sold in bulk.

Illuminations
800-CANDLES
www.illuminations.com
Sensational collection of candles.

## FRESH FLOWERS (INCLUDING
## WHOLESALE CUT FLOWERS
## AND GROWERS' BUNCHES)

Chelsea Wholesale Flower Market
New York, NY
212-620-7500
The fresh flower source for any bride
living in the region.

Costco
800-774-2678
www.costco.com
Visit Costco for affordable bulk
fresh flowers.

eFlower Wholesale
800-255-2640
www.eflowerwholesale.com
This online flower market offers cut
flowers, greens, and floral supplies.

Flowerbud
877-524-5400
www.flowerbud.com
Specializes in fresh cut flowers straight
from growers' fields and greenhouses.

L.A. Flower District
766 Wall Street
Los Angeles, CA
www.laflowerdistrict.com
LA's premier resource for floral design.

San FranciscoFlower Mart
www.sfflmart.com
Great fresh flowers and greenery.

24 Roses
877-U-SEND-24
www.24roses.com
A great source of "direct-from-the-
grower" roses, tulips, and lilies.

## FLORAL DESIGNERS
See also American Institute of Floral
Designers (under Associations).

Big Rose
877-701-7673
www.bigrose.com
Specializes in bridal kits featuring all
your wedding's floral needs, from
boutonnières to bridesmaids' bouquets.

Bridal Blooms & Creations
972-907-8804
www.bridal blooms.com
Sophisticated floral design.

The Knot
www.theknot.com/flowers
Search this bridal site for a lcoal florist.

Martha Stewart Flowers
www.flowers-by-martha.com
Affordable fresh flowers designed by
wedding authority Martha Stewart,
available online, nationwide.

PlantShop
800-729-2213
www.plantshop.com
Flower arrangements, decorative plants,
and containers online.

ProFlowers
800-776-3569
www.proflowers.com
Wide selection of bouquets available
online, including roses awarded "best
value" by the *Wall Street Journal*.

Phillip's 1-800-FLORALS
800-356-7257
www.800florals.com
Purveyor of quality bouquets since 1923.

Romantic Flowers
206-250-8228
www.romanticflowers.com
Wedding flowers are the specialty
of this romantic site.

2G Roses
800-880-0735
www.freshroses.com
Great prices from this "direct-from-the
grower" online florist.

The Wedding Channel
www.weddingchannel.com
Listings for all categories of quality
local wedding vendors, including
floral designers.

U.S. Retail Flowers, Inc.
800-462-5465
www.usretailflowers.com
From romantic roses to novelty gift
baskets nationwide.

PRESERVATION
These companies will preserve your
bouquet professionally for the perfect
keepsake. Options include freeze-drying,
pressing, or silver sand and silica gel.

Aiko & Company
888-245-6626
www.pressed-bouquet.com

The Floral Portrait
800-771-7560
www.thefloralportrait.com

Floral Techniques
408-266-2425
www.floraltechniques.com

Heller & Reid
800-742-9570
www.hellerandreid.com

# picture credits

Key: a=above, b=below, r=right, l=left, c=center.

All photographs by Carolyn Barber unless otherwise stated.

**Craig Fordham**
Pages 2, 6, 8, 10bl, 10bc, 10–11a, 12, 13, 14, 15, 16, 17, 18,
19, 42, 43, 44ar, 44br, 45l, 46a, 46br, 47, 48, 49l, 49ar, 63al,
63bl, 64, 65bl, 66a all, 67r both.
**Polly Wreford**
Pages 1, 5, 9, 10al, 10–11b, 44l, 45r all, 46bl, 46bc, 49cr, 49br,
61, 62, 63ar, 62br, 65al, 65r, 66b, 67l, 78, 79, 80, 81, 82, 83,
84, 85, 86, 87, 106, 107, 108, 110, 112.

With thanks to Carrie Gellin for hand modeling.
Thanks to Ma Maison, 243 Fulham Road, London SW3 6HZ
(+44 20 7371 7573) for the loan of the chair pictured on pages
102–103.

# acknowledgments

I would like to thank Anne-Marie Bulat for giving me the
opportunity to create a book of my wedding flower designs, and
for all her encouragement throughout the project. She made the
photoshoots very relaxed and great fun. Thanks also to the rest of
the RPS team for all their help. I would also like to thank Carolyn
Barber for all her hard work and determination. She is an amazing
photographer.

Thanks to my mum, Betty, for all her patience and help. She has
been an inspiration to me throughout my career, and without her
I could not have achieved this book.

And lastly thanks to my husband for all his encouragement and
ideas and for being so supportive.

Nancy Ursell